W9-ASD-477

THE BELGIAN HORSE

By Sara Green

Consultant:
Dr. Emily Leuthner
DVM, MS, DACVIM
Country View Veterinary Service
Oregon, Wisc.

BELLWETHER MEDIA • MINNEAPOLIS, MN

Jump into the cockpit and take flight with Pilot Books. Your journey will take you on high-energy adventures as you learn about all that is wild, weird, fascinating, and fun!

This edition first published in 2012 by Bellwether Media, Inc.

No part of this publication may be reproduced in whole or in part without written permission of the publisher. For information regarding permission, write to Bellwether Media, Inc., Attention: Permissions Department, 5357 Penn Avenue South, Minneapolis, MN 55419.

Library of Congress Cataloging-in-Publication Data

Green, Sara, 1964-
The Belgian horse / by Sara Green.
    p. cm. – (Pilot books. horse breed roundup)
Includes bibliographical references and index.
  Summary: "Engaging images accompany information about the Belgian Horse. The combination of high-interest subject matter and narrative text is intended for students in grades 3 through 7"–Provided by publisher.
  ISBN 978-1-60014-736-4 (hardcover : alk. paper)
  1. Belgian draft horse–Juvenile literature. I. Title.
SF293.B4G74 2012
636.1'5–dc23
                                    2011028863

Printed in the United States of America, North Mankato, MN.

010112   1204

CONTENTS

The Belgian Horse

A team of two large Belgian horses clops into the competition ring. The crowd watches from the sidelines as 15,000 pounds (6,800 kilograms) of stones are loaded onto a sled. The powerful Belgians pull the heavy load over 20 feet (6 meters) and win the competition! Belgians can pull more weight than almost any other horse breed in the world. They are known as "gentle giants" for their massive size and friendly **temperament**.

Belgians are **draft horses**. Before the engine was invented, many people depended on Belgians to help them do work. Belgians pulled plows on farms and hauled timber out of forests. Firefighters used teams of Belgians, called **hitches**, to pull fire wagons to burning buildings.

The Belgian is among the largest, tallest horse breeds in the world. Most Belgians stand between 16 and 18 **hands** high at the **withers**. This is about 5 to 6 feet (1.5 to 1.8 meters) tall. Belgians have short, muscular necks, wide **girths**, and broad backs. Their shoulders and **hindquarters** are strong and powerful. Their hooves are large and wide. Belgians usually weigh between 1,800 and 2,200 pounds (815 and 1,000 kilograms). The largest Belgian in the world weighed 3,200 pounds (1,452 kilograms)!

roan

Most Belgians have chestnut coats with blond or reddish manes and tails. Chestnut Belgians are copper in color. Other coat colors include gray, roan, and black. Roan coats have white hairs mixed with another color. It is common for Belgians to have white markings called socks on their legs and **blazes** on their noses.

A National Treasure

The **ancestors** of the Belgian breed were Flemish horses. These large black horses lived in an area of Europe called Brabant. Today this area is in the country of Belgium. Rain fell often in Brabant, and the grass grew tall and lush. With plenty of food to eat, the horses became very large and strong. People called them "Great Horses" because of their size. Armored knights rode them into battle during the **Middle Ages**. In time, the Great Horses came to be known as Brabant horses or Belgian horses. People stopped using them as warhorses and began to use them for farm work. These strong workhorses became so popular in Europe that the Belgian government considered them national treasures.

A Giant Appetite
A Belgian eats about 40 pounds (18 kilograms) of grain, grass, and hay in a day. It also drinks about 20 gallons (76 liters) of water per day!

People brought the first Belgians to the United States in the late 1800s. At this time, many Americans were moving west. They needed the strong Belgians to pull wagons and plow the ground for crops. In 1887, the American Association of Importers and Breeders of Belgian Draft Horses was formed to keep track of the breed. Today it is known as the Belgian Draft Horse Corporation of America (BDHCA).

In 1903, Belgium sent a group of Belgian horses to the World's Fair in St. Louis, Missouri. The Belgians drew a lot of interest from the large crowds. However, many people thought the thick, sturdy horses were unattractive. American breeders chose the slimmest Belgians with the longest legs to have **foals**. These foals grew up to have slimmer bodies and longer legs than the European Belgians. People called them American Belgians. They became very popular draft horses on farms across the country.

In the 1940s and 1950s, many farmers replaced their draft horses with tractors. By 1950, the number of new Belgians **registered** in the United States dropped to around 200 horses per year. Fortunately, Belgians made a comeback. Farmers appreciated that the gentle horses were hard workers. They saw that Belgians were less destructive to soil than tractors. The horses also provided **manure**, which is a good **fertilizer**.

Soon, many farmers were once again using Belgians. The number of Belgian horses began to rise. During the early 1980s, the BDHCA registered around 20,000 Belgians born in the U.S. These were great years for the Belgian horse. Today, 3,000 to 4,000 new Belgians are registered every year.

Mighty Pullers

Many of today's Belgians show off their great strength in competitions. The powerful horses are at their best when they pull heavy loads. Belgian horses often dominate horse pulling. Local farmers started this sport. They would challenge one another to see whose horse could pull the most weight. Over time, horse pulling became a popular sport across the country.

In horse pulling, teams of horses are fitted with **harnesses**. They are then hitched either to sleds loaded with weights or to a **dynamometer**. The team that can pull the most weight over a set distance wins the competition.

Belgians begin to train for pulling contests when they are 4 years old. Trainers help the horses build their strength. At first, horses pull light loads. They pull heavier loads as their strength increases.

Forty Strong

One of the most famous Belgian teams was Dick Sparrow's 40-horse hitch. He lined the horses up in 10 rows with 4 horses in each row. The horses stretched out for 120 feet (37 meters) in front of the carriage. In the 1970s, Dick Sparrow took his 40-horse hitch to events across the country. People were impressed that so many Belgians could work together as a team.

Have you ever seen a hitch of Belgians pulling a carriage or a wagon? With their braided manes and large hooves, the towering Belgians are an impressive sight. Many people get their first view of a Belgian hitch at a parade or circus. Belgian hitches often pull special show wagons. These wagons are usually restored **antiques** with elaborate designs. Many drivers wear old-fashioned clothes and hats.

One of the most exciting places to watch Belgians is at hitch competitions. In these events, teams of up to eight Belgians are hitched to wagons. As drivers guide their teams around a **show ring**, judges give the horses points for teamwork, gracefulness, behavior, and appearance. The teams make the ground tremble when they move around the show ring!

17

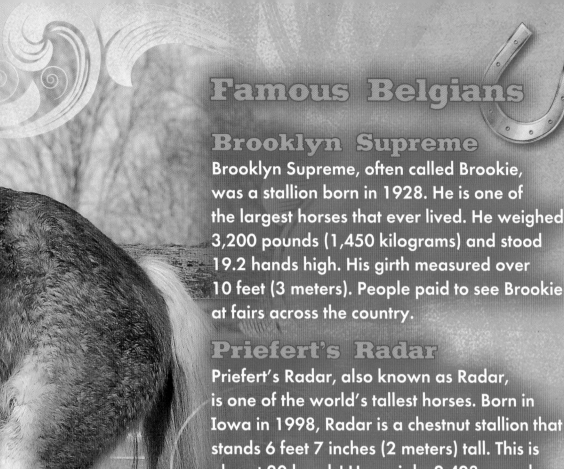

Famous Belgians

Brooklyn Supreme

Brooklyn Supreme, often called Brookie, was a stallion born in 1928. He is one of the largest horses that ever lived. He weighed 3,200 pounds (1,450 kilograms) and stood 19.2 hands high. His girth measured over 10 feet (3 meters). People paid to see Brookie at fairs across the country.

Priefert's Radar

Priefert's Radar, also known as Radar, is one of the world's tallest horses. Born in Iowa in 1998, Radar is a chestnut stallion that stands 6 feet 7 inches (2 meters) tall. This is almost 20 hands! He weighs 2,423 pounds (1,100 kilograms). Radar's owners bring him to fairs and exhibits around the United States to give people a chance to see him.

McIlrath's Captain Jim

McIlrath's Captain Jim is listed in the Guinness Book of World Records as the most expensive draft horse ever sold. The two-year-old stallion sold for $112,500 at the Mid-America Draft Horse Sale in Gifford, Illinois in 2003. His value came from remarkable bloodlines from both his mother and father.

The Belgian breed has a wonderful success story. For centuries, it was a popular workhorse. When farming practices changed in the middle of the twentieth century, Belgians faced tough times. However, their strength, friendly nature, and willingness to work helped their numbers come back strong.

Today the breed is as popular as ever. Farmers all over the world rely on Belgians to plow fields and pull wagons. Belgians are some of the most popular features at parades and circuses. Many people also enjoy riding Belgians for fun. It may take a helpful boost to get into the saddle, but the smooth, comfortable ride of a Belgian is worth the effort. It's no surprise that the strong, gentle Belgian is America's most popular draft horse!

Glossary

ancestors—family members who lived long ago

antiques—objects that were made long ago

blazes—white marks on the noses of horses

draft horses—large, tall horses used for heavy physical labor

dynamometer—a machine used in horse pulling contests to measure horsepower

fertilizer—a substance added to soil that helps plants grow

foals—young horses; foals are under one year old.

girths—the distances around the bellies of animals

hands—the units used to measure the height of a horse; one hand is equal to 4 inches (10.2 centimeters).

harnesses—sets of straps attached to animals to help them pull carriages or wagons

hindquarters—the hind legs and muscles of a four-legged animal

hitches—teams of horses attached together with harnesses and chains in order to pull a carriage or wagon

manure—the waste of animals; manure is often used as fertilizer.

Middle Ages—a period in Europe that lasted from the 500s to the 1500s

registered—made record of; owners register their horses with official breed organizations.

show ring—the ring where horses compete and are displayed at a horse show

temperament—personality or nature; the Belgian has a friendly temperament.

withers—the ridge between the shoulder blades of a horse

To Learn More

At the Library

Hendricks, Bonnie L. *International Encyclopedia of Horse Breeds.* Norman, Okla.: University of Oklahoma Press, 2007.

Maas, Sarah. *The Belgian Horse.* Mankato, Minn.: Capstone Press, 2006.

Peterson, Cris. *Horsepower: The Wonder of Draft Horses.* Honesdale, Pa.: Boyds Mills Press, 2001.

On the Web

Learning more about Belgian horses is as easy as 1, 2, 3.

1. Go to www.factsurfer.com

2. Enter "Belgian horses" into the search box.

3. Click the "Surf" button and you will see a list of related Web sites.

With factsurfer.com, finding more information is just a click away.

Index